Songs From the Mountaintop

Kassandra Dick

BookLeaf Publishing

India | USA | UK

Presentation by *BookLeaf Publishing*

Web: www.bookleafpub.com

E-mail: info@bookleafpub.com

ISBN: 9789357618717

First edition 2022

To my parents, Tina and Ron, without whom,

I would never have known what love is meant to feel like.

To the great philosopher, Ayn Rand, without whom,

I would never have known what life is meant to be.

How Did I Get Here?

At the top of the mountain
I must retrace my steps

Remember which trails, boulders,
and rock shoulders corralled me in

Today, a friend rallied me to ask,
Why do I believe reality has laws?

What makes me so sure
I can know them?
Hone them?
Own them?

My question is, why don't I
fold to wishes, whims, or Gods?

I have only my teachers to thank.
I thank myself for the climb

Am I Certain?

"Nothing is certain," he says,
puffs out his chest and in the same breath,
"I can't even be sure you exist."

I look straight into his eyes
"You should just ask me."

"How would I know you aren't lying?"

"How could I lie if I don't exist?"

These are the answers
Kantians don't want to give
They want to believe this
could all be a figment

Makes it easier to sleep with a nihilist–
You keep your victimhood intact

How can you be wrong
if there are no cold, hard facts?

It's easy to fold, if you're constantly told
there's nothing besides the confines of hivemind
So? Compromise.

Follow the leader, fall off the cliff
Wallow in the waterhole of skeptics

Is this the reality you paid for?
Where the truth is made up
and the facts don't matter?

Or
Will you use your brain like a laser
Align your sights to find solutions
Empower yourself with what you know
because you do know

be it by trial and error
through observation
through experience
but above all, by reason

Consciousness
is a thankless process
The thinker
is the only one who benefits

It Starts at a Young Age

Self-denial is so delicious

When you're good at it
you can pretend
Someone else will take the wheel–
It doesn't even matter
if I drive or die

It's just me, myself and Inquisitor

Please criticize–
make me taste okay–
to the greatest number

Please
tone me down to the deaf masses
make me sound sweet
Make me sweat over beat
Make me bleed

only to see
my sacrifice
is not enough

No sacrifice can be.

Only what we choose to keep
can truly give us peace

Only who we choose to be
Can truly make us free

Growing Up

We run half our lives
on someone else's time
Then we wonder
Where the hell was I?

We question ourselves
first

then our teachers
find out, why—

Who did I turn to?
What did I try?

Faith
was never the man
Reason is

Reason is a hand extended
reaching past ripples
of hopes and prayers

Faith
is a breath held
while your ship launches

Reason
is the blood, sweat, and gears

Focus

Failure
can only steer you
into learning

Death
can only scare you
into living

Hold That Thought

Can you?

Can you cling
to a full stop?

Reach
the conclusion

Find
the solution

and move on.

Why not?

What stands between mind and complete
thought?
Give it time. Even when you stop stirring the pot

the stew takes a moment to settle

Settle for nothing
short of the whole story

Now thought. No

thought. New thought.
Now

Fluid motion through
preconceived notions

Never getting caught up in the spin

Think
in pure open space

Learn
from unlimited mistakes

Speak
truth like you like the taste

Live
the life you don't have to escape

Under/water

There are no harder words to form
 than "I love myself"

Anything other than self-deprecation
feels narcissistic when
you're not the one drowning

I keep trying to send love
like a message in a bottle
but I'm up to my waist
my shoulders
my throat

Maybe if I save them
I can love myself
Maybe if they love me
we can save each other

but I've tried
to find myself in the lighthouse
and the shipwreck

There is no us at all
when we're up against the waves

So I breathe in and relax
Maybe
for the first time in my life
Let the waters bring me back to shore

Of course
How could an s.o.s go out
when the tide is pulling in?

I lie still on the sand
and in the first full breaths
I hear my own blood in my ears

The only heartbeat I know
and I owe my life to it

Honor the being within
that is willing to love thyself

Trust in the mind
a little more at a time

In the Mirror

I start with my eyes
I reassure myself I am safe
in that stare, in that state

I trust what I see
and it's all there. I am safe
with myself
as myself
in this body

In this moment
I see the line across my stomach
where the top half settles on the bottom
I remind myself that I am made
of sweet treats, green leaves,
juicy, crunchy, savory things

I see my chest tremble
see my nipples sprawl
totally at ease

I resist the urge to tease

I take a deep breath in
and rely on my beauty. Not what others

tell me beauty is. This is supreme being

This is me
This is who I have become
in the struggle, but beyond the need
to be
any way at all

My jaw softens naturally
My thighs roll out
I see the legs that have carried me
Through the mud and the storm and the trees

I see my sex
so tender to the touch
So free

To exact my body
To be exactly here

Myself

I will never exist
somewhere else
Not on the scale,
nor in the mirror
I
am
here

Body of Space

Look at these precious beings

Us!

Each in a body like a fortress

A body that can take
pressure and stress
and point
to tenderness
not
rigidness

Kindness
not mindless obedience
spontaneous circuitry
powered and propelled by
open intelligence

Body is not robot
Body is machine
created to operate infinity
Body is born so that God needn't be

Body dies

because God can't

God can only borrow our blueprint of being
Through the tectonic and technological
freedom of sensation and motion and speech

for each of us
because each God gets used
to their place of worship, their unique form
with atomic specifications nobody asked for

the injuries we can't ignore
the illnesses we can't afford

We
read the manual
We
become compatible

to whatever our DNA
had to work with that day

Body isn't always preset to Our tastes
the way We ache
what makes Us quiver and quake

Each temple is equal
though not always symmetrical
never identical, yet all the same

in a fundamental way

Our bodies contain space

Our minds expand it

so that this present moment
pulses with electric potential

yet simultaneously
remains stable
to the pinpoint
of perfection

Spiral into perfect love
of body

The same way
you spiral into love
as soon as a baby
holds your pinky
like a promise

Promise your body!

We are in this together
and we are in this all the way

Peace of Mind

Panic

and the mind dies

or

Under static pressure
resist the urge
to crack

Stretched beyond kinetic stress
refuse to snap back
into nothingness

To be is to desire to be?

No

To be is to be

I desire to be
electrified
alive and wired

Lightning mind!

Still
victory
relies on

stillness

I rely on potential energy

Reality flips the switch
and truth tears through arteries
only

Wisdom
rushes in like oxygen

Trust enlivened mind
for the love of Guru
Listen to her Anthem
Hear the hum? Her words
like blood

The thrumming heart
and pumping lungs
the cry that builds

from stillness

You were made for this

Now BE!

Not to be
is still a possibility

Not to think
was never an option

No matter what you're faced with
You can always choose to be
at peace

How to Win A Fight

Step one. Start a fight

What might
be the end game though?
Is your pain still yours alone?

Own your time. Own your mind

and You will control
the outcomes of your goals
You cannot control someone else

Learn to make fire
Learn to name fears

Learn to face them
with fists unclenched

Sure, learn to fight,
but not with your friends–
Not with your own mind

Use all of your might for what's right
Freedom of choice, Freedom of voice

Not of the many,
only each one.

Stars amid constellations
We speak *with* one another, never for

With those who are voiceless—
We listen!

to the heartbeat below the pain
the marching feet through bloodied rain
the desperate fear, the rolling tanks
the frost, the muck—we hear them rage

FUCK WAR

No to soldiers on the ground. No
to explosions
property stolen
broken
torched

No to Propo!
Take a gander
at our seamless sphere

SEE THE PEOPLE

here

and here

WE THE LIVING
can still hear the tree fall

To all who would deafen us
To all who would silence us

We see your war machine
and we raise you HELL

No to regimented kindness
No to monitored love

We choose peace
every time we choose
not to fight, but to win

We get in
We start a conversation
We stoke not change,
but progress

Now!
for the love of all that is dear to You
do not rest, where justice is due

If just one human dies
We, of dust and ashes,
Rise

Empowerment

Freedom is not handed out
It grows

Like lotus through the muck
through the filth and the lies

If you despise the one-size–
fit your fist to the sky

Feel the space above you?
Take it

Feel the growth within you?
Trust it

If you have no choice
you have no freedom

every package deal
comes with a hidden price

Man pays for free will with his life

I Make Time for Myself

Not, as I used to say,
"So I can give more to others."
This is my time on earth
This is my headspace

I don't owe for being here
I don't have to make a name
I have to stake a claim to this body

In this soul
I grow older. Every day
I break the mold
I take a hold of my own hand

and give thanks to myself for once

It's so easy to give me up
to something–
anything–
Greater than

I make time for myself
because whether I like it or not,
I cannot be the greatest
unless I'm the best I've got

Meditation on Death

I live like I am being watched
because I am
I am watching this life unfold
It is mine, yet not mine alone

It is divine,
for it's my sole opportunity
to breathe
soul into body
Possibility into being

Before you die
you do watch your life go by

It's only a flash
if you never look with your own eyes

The Thing About Magic

Let's say you note the sharp stick
poking out of a woodpile

You foresee

It will make contact
with somebody's eye
but there's still time

To change the future,
you remove the obstacle
You become oracle hero
Ganesha in the flesh

Let's say, you see the wound
someone is trying to compress
With love in your voice,
you hold space for them to heal
You feel like Jesus in blue jeans

You heard what he said,
As below, so in the head
Using the mind *is* magic
doesn't rely on the fantastic

Rely on your open intelligence
fully formed, radically present
ready to do what reality requires

Man takes sticks and stones
and makes fire

The Thing About Math

You don't *have* to do it
Calculators exist
but the ones who program computers
are who you have to thank

The ones who save your skin
knowing the difference in inches
between your face and the airbag
your foot and the edge…

Shout out to engineers and architects

Math wasn't just sitting around
waiting to be turned over in our hands
Not like the blocks you and I played with

One need only apply equations
to any human problem
and witness mind
over magic

, it's true,

On the cusp of CRISPR
and nano-regen technologies
it is imperative to critically consider
the prolonged vitality of our species

I'm not talking postcard happiness, here people
I'm talking long, drawn out lives,
aided and abetted by bionic limbs
and espresso machines that know your decision
six seconds before you do

You can't pretend
you are getting too old for technology
Technology is seeping into your dreams
It's creeping into your cornflakes
like those little bits of iron
slipped in to meet the daily
recommended requirements

How soon until we reach optimal intake?
How long until the cancer jig is up
and we are faced, not with our deadliest
advisory, heart disease,
but instead, our greatest achievement
the juice cleanse of youth

Now is the time to stop speculating
Stop reprinting Oryx and Crake
You cannot compute this utopian present
because your history book is from 1984

Ours is no longer a game
of hidden lives and thought crimes
Instead of collective mobs
gobbling up genius, electing slobs

We, as individuals,
create an era of great benefit.

We will outlive our parents
We will outgrow our planet
We, who hold the knowledge
of the universe in a usable way,

And so?

Impudence

It's not like a poem
to have an opinion

much like a woman,
one should be seen
yet remain

contained in patient restraint

I've let sleeping lines lie
for far too long

Now this poem wants
to scream
but like water
It flows on—
so softly

no one can hear
the thunder below

Give praise to the poem
Who outlasts silence

Indifference

Hate

This poem is done praying.
I tried to keep quiet
but pain is a triumph

Freedom is
atom bomb
YOU MUST
split humanity
Into humans

You must take–
Freedom cannot be given

Speaking up for yourself
does not harm someone else.

This poem cannot speak for all women
but it speaks out for all people

Suffer, and death becomes a gift

Live, and it's the
ultimate test

Trust

is built on granite
Sandstone after a rain
breaks apart in your hand
like a smile once the love is gone

Trust
feels like building a fire
Even after the rain
the tinder can spark
you can nurture the flame

Trust what your hands have made
Shape yourself after the rain
Notice, what gets washed away?
Look, what remains?

Trust in the light of your mind
Take time to practice being okay
with everything, all at once
just for a short moment

Just in yourself,
for one short moment

Trust

A Child is Conceived

When it is wondered about
When it is dreamt of
When it is wanted
When it is loved

Let all be born in love
Let all know a life
of intention

Of hand held to belly
with warmth in palm
of calm happiness
pressed upon forehead
like a blessing

Yes
I am ready
think the ones
who will hold this tiny heart

Yes
I can guide you
say all who would treasure this mind

Children are not created by force

They become themselves
regardless of who raises them

Let them come into the home
when it is made for them,
and not a moment before

Potential Poetry

There are no rights past what the writer can offer
A rapist cannot make me carry his words to term
A preacher cannot fill my womb with a sermon
A politician wishes his speeches were fertile

They are wasting OUR breath

A poem can die a thousand ways
while we all point the picket signs

A writer has to love life enough to say,
I cannot do this poem justice

so I will learn
from what I have erased

My lack of sacrifice is not in vain

For this poem may
have a life of its own
Where it will go
I have no say

Without me
these words won't survive

Without choice,
neither will I

Sex Cake

To engender a cake
begin with basic ingredients
flour, sugar, oil
but even those will be contested

Our sources and proportions
should inform identity
but there are different names
for the same pastry

Will this be a happy birthday cake—
or one shoved down our throats?

Before we layer on les normes du gâteau
We have to ask, why does it matter
if I make marble or crumb?

It matters to the one who isn't safe
walking their cake to school
It matters to the one who is shamed
for not appearing on the menu

Rather than rip up our recipes
we make new

We teach children to whisk for themselves
We teach the risks of taking a cake out too soon

We celebrate taste. Critics haven't got a clue
You cannot have your cake and eat mine too

Money is Free

All you do
is work for it
or trade for it
or invest

Free does not mean
Guaranteed

You must
work for it
or trade for it
or invest

Time is money
Your every minute

worth exactly
what you put in it

Free Speech

Doesn't mean "Free Stage"
You earn attention
or you pay

Get rich wagering

celebrity
with respect

Power over
empowerment

Take media coverage away
from the wars religions wage
Blame the Jews...again

Pay money for trivial deals
YOU MADE
Fade
like a passing craze

Ye,

Speech has never been so free
If only we

can focus, if only

We can keep the streams live
so their screams don't die

Battle Call

If the pen is to be mightier,
then my word needs to be heavier
I must lift my voice to the sky

Every time tyranny tries
tearing us apart
we sprawl

The pen may be mighty, but peace is slow
The sword swings doors closed

So we break walls
We relay the call
not by little tin cans
but by cables spanning oceans

We don't buy news, we pay attention
We don't fight the weak for their pen

The sword swings swiftly
bleeds our constitution
till we risk running out of ink
We hold on

Freedom is never said and done
Peace is declared yet the sword swings on

If The Truth Hurts

If the truth hurts, ask yourself why

Did you stub your toe trying to evade it?

Did you lose yourself in the maze
you made in your mind?

Was the story you told getting old,
or did you forget the moral by the twentieth
time?

We can only ever face the truth

a bone may break without a bruise
We can play again even when we lose

Even when confused
it never hurts to say,

"My mistake."

"I didn't realize."

"Thank you for letting me know."

Although the ego likes
to get it right the first time

we relax the need to know it all
and see?

It was only growing pains

God

once spelled good,
it was the deed
of the living

Devil, once spelled evil,
was nonentity—

a bad choice

Man
makes choices

now. Make Your Choice
See God(s) and Devil(s) OR

Reality

Look
into the sun and be
blinded by divine radiance
or by radiation

Whatever You choose, You DO
and reality does not care. You DO
God does not exist. You DO

The Son
is not the answer

The answer
is within

Mind
frees man from myth
and we evolve

Magic
dissolves
into mist and shards

Math
dispels dishonesty

Science
delves into mystery

History is. Learn from it

Existence exists
Consciousness is conscious of it

You are, so see
You judge, so be!

The good in your life
is Your responsibility.

Ah, men

We Do Not Play God

We are Gods
playing with reality
The way we were meant to be
The way only *we* can

The only way we can

Some like playing man
like it's inherently bad
to say with conviction
Our future's not science fiction

We own this planet
but it is only our first

Human
is not a dirty word.

We are pure
as in
free from anything of a different kind
Free to use rational mind

Mankind is a gift
we must offer ourselves

For we deserve

peace and prosperity
happiness and liberty

and We Shall Have It

Ye shall have
all the life ye can muster

You do not have to suffer
to be good. You were born into it
Anyone who speaks of original sin
would sell your soul to a bookclub

Circumstance gave you consciousness
Only you can break the yolk
For the love of Man, stop paying lip service

To the father,
the son,
and the holy hoax

Life Goals

I don't care about power
I'm not driven by greed
all I'm in for
is prestige

For myself first,
and humanity
not because I'd die
for any man out there,
but I live for all the noble,
proud, and brave

I live for a future where freedom
means more than birdshit
on the back of a pick up—

Where fate
isn't a game

Where fame
isn't a given

Where time stops for no
poet and if I want this,
I must create
my role on the stage

I have to wager the time
it takes for me to do
what I mean to
with the time I have left alive

I'm not the first with this kind of pride
but I am the first with this kind of drive

I will live like I love every minute of it
I will be my own biggest fan

The Happiest

I've felt for a long time
is not the happiest I've been,
nor to say, I'll ever be
This happiness is combined
with the wisdom

It ain't a given

It's a fine line
between been there/
done that

I don't have to go back
to depression, that cat can
rest easy. I put enough pressure
on my own chest without risking
my breathing

I don't want to say I'll never lay low again
I might still today. The happiness tho
is acquired knowledge, accumulated good

The values I keep, the lessons I've understood
Happiness is not a method, it is a result
The method is one moment at a time

Where do I Go?

In time, I look back at the wall
that once seemed too tall to scale

I trace the trails of my teachers then on I forge
and rejoice!
for there is further still to go

My journey will end
but I do not lament the road
less traveled

I refuse regret
fear was merely my compass
I go where I can and I understand

Limits exist.

My comfort zone may be malleable
but my boundaries are staked in
My heart may be in the right place
but I learn when I'm mistaken

All I know is I cannot grow
without goals
without freedom

I grant myself
the serenity
the courage
and the wisdom